J 352.23097 KELLAHER
Kellaher, Karen
The Presidency

WITHDRAWN

022222

Why It Matters

The Presidency

Karen Kellaher

Children's Press®
An Imprint of Scholastic Inc.

Content Consultant
Saikrishna Bangalore Prakash
James Monroe Distinguished Professor of Law
Paul G. Mahoney Research Professor of Law
Miller Center Senior Fellow
University of Virginia
Charlottesville, Virginia

Teacher Adviser
Rachel Hsieh

Library of Congress Cataloging-in-Publication Data
Names: Kellaher, Karen, author.
Title: The Presidency: Why It Matters to You / Karen Kellaher.
Description: New York : Children's Press, an imprint of Scholastic, Inc., 2020. | Series: A true book. Why it
    matters | Includes bibliographical references and index.
Identifiers: LCCN 2019004802 | ISBN 9780531231852 (library binding) | ISBN 9780531239971 (pbk.)
Subjects: LCSH: Presidents—United States—Juvenile literature. | United States—Politics and government—
    Juvenile literature.
Classification: LCC JK517 .K45 2020 | DDC 352.230973—dc23
LC record available at https://lccn.loc.gov/2019004802

All rights reserved. Published in 2020 by Children's Press, an imprint of Scholastic Inc.
Printed in North Mankato, MN, USA 113

SCHOLASTIC, CHILDREN'S PRESS, A TRUE BOOK™, and associated logos are trademarks and/or
registered trademarks of Scholastic Inc.

Scholastic Inc., 557 Broadway, New York, NY 10012

2 3 4 5 6 7 8 9 10 R 29 28 27 26 25 24 23 22 21 20

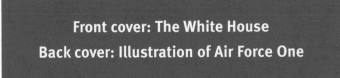

Front cover: The White House
Back cover: Illustration of Air Force One

Find the Truth!

Everything you are about to read is true *except* for one of the sentences on this page.

Which one is **TRUE**?

T or F One president kept a pet raccoon at the White House.

T or F You can run for president once you turn 21 years old.

Find the answers in this book.

Contents

The donkey and the elephant are symbols of the United States' two main political parties.

The BIG Truth

More Than Two Terms?

4 Inside the Presidency

The presidential seal

Think About It!

Take a close look at the room pictured in this photo. It may seem ordinary, but it is the spot where some of our nation's most important decisions are made. It is the White House Oval Office, where the U.S. president works. Where do you think presidents get their power? How do the president's decisions affect you? Why does it matter to you?

Intrigued?
Want to know more? Turn the page!

The U.S. Constitution laid out the nation's system of government.

Creating a Government

Imagine you have to plan a government for a new country. You want a strong government, but you also want to make sure that no person or group is too powerful.

That was the challenge facing the writers of the U.S. Constitution in 1787. The United States had recently won its independence from Great Britain. The writers decided to make a government with three branches, or parts. Each branch would limit the power of the others.

The legislative branch is made up of the U.S. Congress, which includes the House of Representatives and the Senate. Congress writes the nation's laws. The judicial branch, led by the U.S. Supreme Court, interprets those laws. The president leads the executive branch, which makes sure laws are carried out.

The U.S. president works with other members of the executive branch and with the other two branches to keep the nation running smoothly. The president's decisions affect everything from the economy to the environment.

President William H. Taft (1909–1913) sits at his White House desk.

Barack Obama was the nation's first African American president.

President Barack Obama (2009–2017) greets crowds after winning the 2008 presidential election. His family is by his side.

Could You Be President?

If there were an ad for the job of president, it might say: "WANTED: Leader of a diverse nation of 325 million citizens. You must be willing to live in Washington, D.C., work long hours, and make difficult decisions. Position is for a **term** of four years. A second term is possible." Would you apply for this job? In some ways, the road to the presidency is as challenging as the job itself!

Requirements for the Job

The Constitution gives three requirements for being president. You must be at least 35 years old. You must have lived in the United States for at least 14 years. And you must be a "natural born citizen," or born in the United States or to U.S. citizens.

The country's presidents have been lawyers, farmers, military generals, business leaders, and even actors. Many have held other government positions, such as governors of states or lawmakers in the U.S. Congress.

Before serving as president, Abraham Lincoln (1861–1865) had many jobs, including woodcutter, store clerk, and lawyer.

Cartoonists often use a donkey to stand for the Democratic Party and an elephant to stand for the Republican Party. In this cartoon, how are these animals dressed? What colors and shapes do you see on their clothing? Why do you think they are dressed like this?

Ready, Set, Run!

Voters help choose the U.S. president in an election every four years. The people running for president are called candidates. They **campaign** to convince people they are right for the job. Candidates also pick a running mate, who would serve as vice president.

Each candidate represents a political party. This is a group of people with similar ideas about how to run the government. Most candidates today belong to either the Democratic or the Republican Party. Others may belong to the Green, the Independent, or other smaller parties.

U.S. Electoral Votes by State
(as of 2019)

WA 12
OR 7
ID 4
MT 3
ND 3
MN 10
WY 3
SD 3
WI 10
MI 16
NV 6
UT 6
CO 9
NE 5
IA 6
NM 5
AZ 11
CA 55
KS 6
MO 10
OK 7
AR 6
TX 34
LA 8
MS 6
AL 9
GA 16
IL 20
IN 11
OH 18
KY 8
TN 11
WV 5
VA 13
NC 15
SC 9
FL 29
PA 20
NJ 14
DE 3
MD 10
DC 3
NY 29
VT 3
NH 4
MA 11
RI 4
CT 7
ME 4
AK 3
HI 4

This map shows how many electoral votes each state has.

Kids can sometimes join their parents in the voting booth.

The Winner Is . . .

On Election Day in November, millions of Americans cast ballots. This is called the popular vote. The winner of the popular vote in each state will usually get that state's **electoral votes**. Each state has a certain number of electoral votes based in part on population. There are 538 electoral votes in all. A candidate must win at least 270 to become president.

Taking an Oath

The newly elected candidate officially becomes president on **Inauguration** Day in January. Presidents take the Oath of Office in a ceremony outside the U.S. Capitol in Washington, D.C. This oath is a promise to serve and protect the country. Then the president gives a speech outlining important goals for the nation. You can watch the event in person or on TV.

President George Washington (1789–1797) was inaugurated in New York, where the captial was at the time.

New York City was the nation's capital from April 1789 to July 1790.

President Franklin D. Roosevelt's third inaugural parade

First Day Festivities

After the inauguration ceremony, the new president, vice president, and their families lead a parade down Pennsylvania Avenue. This street connects the Capitol, where the inauguration takes place, to the White House, where the president will live. The parade includes members of the U.S. military and marching bands from all over the country. Later that day, there are parties called inaugural balls. Some presidents have attended 10 or more balls that day!

Next in Line

If a president dies or leaves office, the vice president takes over. As of 2018, this has happened nine times. In eight of those instances, a president died in office. Once, a president resigned, or stepped down.

What if something happens to the vice president too? A law officially lists the people who would take over as president if needed. It includes leaders in Congress and members of the president's cabinet, or group of advisers.

Vice President Lyndon B. Johnson became president after President John F. Kennedy (1961–1963) was assassinated, or killed, in 1963.

17

President George W.
Bush (2001–2009)
speaks to U.S. troops.

With about 1.3 million
troops, the U.S. military
is one of the world's
largest military forces.

A Big Job

You may have heard that "the president wears many hats." That means the president has many important roles in leading the nation. Some of those roles are spelled out in the U.S. Constitution. Others are not mentioned in the Constitution but have developed over time. The many responsibilities make the president the most powerful public official in the country. They also keep the president very busy!

Chief Executive

One of the president's roles is chief executive. The president executes, or carries out, the nation's laws. To help, the president picks people to lead 15 government departments. Each person deals with a different subject, such as agriculture or education, and advises the president. Together with the vice president, they make up the cabinet. The president also appoints **federal** judges, including the justices on the Supreme Court, the nation's top court.

Timeline of Famous Executive Orders

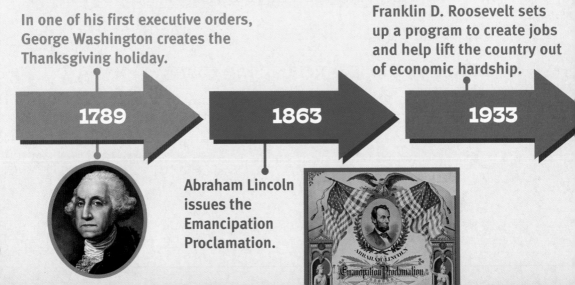

In one of his first executive orders, George Washington creates the Thanksgiving holiday.

Franklin D. Roosevelt sets up a program to create jobs and help lift the country out of economic hardship.

1789

1863

1933

Abraham Lincoln issues the Emancipation Proclamation.

As chief executive, the president can issue executive orders. They are not laws, but they do carry a lot of weight. One famous executive order is the Emancipation Proclamation. President Abraham Lincoln issued it during the Civil War (1861–1865) to free enslaved people in the South.

The president also has the power to **pardon** people found guilty of certain crimes. The president can officially forgive the person and excuse the person from punishment.

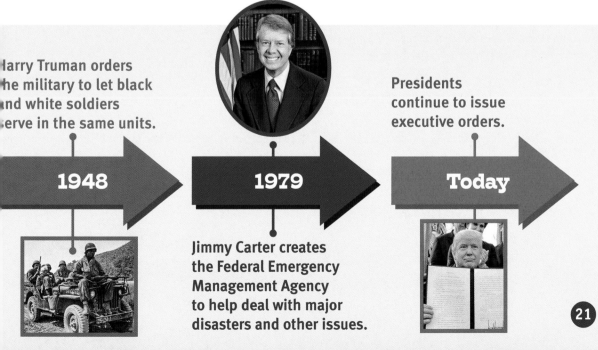

Harry Truman orders the military to let black and white soldiers serve in the same units.

1948

1979

Jimmy Carter creates the Federal Emergency Management Agency to help deal with major disasters and other issues.

Presidents continue to issue executive orders.

Today

This cartoon shows President Harry S. Truman (1945–1953) wearing a military hat that is much too big for him. What opinion do you think the cartoonist had about Truman as the commander in chief?

Troops and Treaties

The president is also the commander in chief, or person in charge, of the U.S. military. Only Congress can declare war. But presidents have sent out troops without a declaration from Congress when there is a crisis or a threat to the country.

In addition, the president is the nation's most important **diplomat**, deciding how the United States deals with other countries. The Constitution allows the president to make **treaties** with other nations with the Senate's approval.

More than half of all U.S. presidents served in the military before they took office.

Laws and Budgets

Congress writes the nation's laws. But the president can suggest ideas for **bills**, or new laws. Once Congress passes a bill, the president has the power to sign it into law or to **veto** (reject) it.

The president is also an economic leader. In that role, the president proposes the U.S. government's budget, which lays out how the country's money will be spent. Congress then reviews and votes on the plan.

President George H. W. Bush (1989–1993) signed the Americans with Disabilities Act into law. It prevents discrimination against people with disabilities.

President Donald Trump and Queen Elizabeth II of the United Kingdom inspect the British Guard of Honor in 2018.

Other Roles

As America's head of state, the president is a symbol of the nation. Presidents greet visiting leaders from other countries and give medals to U.S. heroes. They often carry out patriotic traditions, such as throwing out the first pitch of a Major League Baseball season.

Presidents also lead their political party. In this role, presidents may give speeches to help other politicians in the party get elected.

State of the Union

Can you imagine writing your own report card? In some ways, that's what presidents do! The Constitution requires presidents to report to Congress on how the country is doing, among other topics. Most presidents do this by giving a yearly State of the Union **address**. The speech usually takes place in the U.S. Capitol and airs on TV for everyone to watch. Presidents discuss their accomplishments and share their ideas for improving the country.

In 1995, President Bill Clinton (1993–2001) delivered the longest State of the Union speech on record. It had 9,190 words!

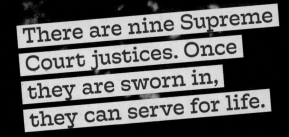

There are nine Supreme Court justices. Once they are sworn in, they can serve for life.

President Ronald Reagan (1981–1989) appointed the first female justice to the U.S. Supreme Court, Sandra Day O'Connor. The U.S. Senate approved the choice.

Checks and Balances

After reading about the president's roles, you might imagine that presidents can do whatever they want. But that's not the case. Each of the three branches of government can check, or limit, the powers of the others. Both Congress and the Supreme Court keep the president from being too powerful. This is known as a system of checks and balances.

The President's Picks

The president appoints many public officials. Heads of government departments and agencies, U.S. **ambassadors**, and federal judges are just a few examples. But there are limits to this power. The U.S. Senate must approve the people the president names for certain jobs. For example, when the president picks a new justice for the U.S. Supreme Court, senators interview the person. They can vote "no" if they don't think the person will do a good job.

NOT A BAD IDEA EH?

LATE SPRING S
To BE W
BY GENTLEM
NOMINATEL
To BE MEMBEI
OF THE
U.S. SUPREME COURT

This 1930 cartoon suggests that a person nominated to the Supreme Court needs to wear protective armor when being questioned by the Senate. What can you guess about this process?

Veto Limits

The president can reject a new law Congress has passed. But that's not necessarily the end of the story! Members of Congress can vote to pass it even without the president's signature. This is

President John Tyler (1841–1845) was the first president to have a veto overridden. The law he tried to stop was about building new Coast Guard ships.

called overriding the president's veto. It is not easy to do. Two-thirds of each part of Congress must vote to override.

That's an Order . . . Or Is It?

As you've read, the president can give executive orders that hold a lot of power. But executive orders have limits too. Imagine if a president gives an order saying that all government employees will get a big raise. If Congress disagrees, it can pass a law that overturns the executive order. The federal courts can also review them. Their judges stop any orders that they believe go against the Constitution or other laws.

The U.S. Supreme Court and other federal courts can stop an executive order.

This drawing shows President Andrew Johnson (1865–1869) at his impeachment trial.

Impeachment

If the House of Representatives believes a president has broken the law, it can vote to charge the president with a high crime. This is called impeachment. Then the Senate holds a trial. The Senate removes the president from office if two-thirds of the senators reach a "guilty" verdict. Three presidents have been impeached: Andrew Johnson, Bill Clinton and Donald Trump. The Senate did not find them guilty, so they remained in office. Richard Nixon resigned when it looked as if he would be impeached.

More Than Two Terms?

The original Constitution did not say anything about how many terms a president could serve. George Washington stepped down after two terms. Most other presidents followed this tradition. One exception was President Franklin D. Roosevelt (1933–1945). He was elected to four terms! In 1951, the 22nd Amendment to the Constitution became law. It said that presidents could be elected to only two terms. But even today, some people disagree with this rule.

What do you think?

This photo of Franklin D. Roosevelt was taken in 1941.

THE WHITE HOUSE
WASHINGTON

Should presidents be allowed to serve more than two terms?

YES	NO
✔ How long an individual president serves should be up to the American people.	✔ A new president usually brings fresh new ideas to the office.
✔ It can take more than two terms for a president to achieve important goals for the nation.	✔ A two-term limit inspires a president to work quickly to accomplish goals.
✔ Sometimes the nation experiences a long war or other crisis. It could help to have the same person lead the nation through the tough time.	✔ The longer a president is in the White House, the harder it is for them to relate to ordinary citizens and the challenges they face.
✔ There are many checks and balances in place to keep a president from becoming too powerful.	✔ Being in office for too long will let a president become too king-like.

It takes 570 gallons (2,158 liters) of white paint to cover the outside of the White House.

Every president except George Washington has lived in the White House.

Inside the Presidency

Being president is not exactly easy. But the job does have many rewards! The president earns $400,000 a year, plus an extra allowance to pay for food and other expenses. The president also has free transportation and around-the-clock bodyguards. And the president gets to live in the White House in Washington, D.C. A president's spouse and children often live in this mansion too. Together, they are called the first family.

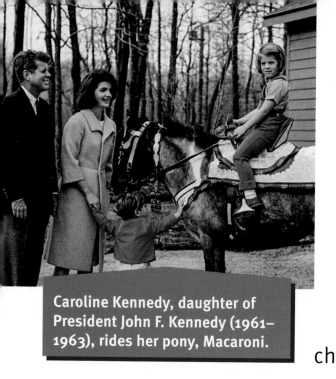

Caroline Kennedy, daughter of President John F. Kennedy (1961–1963), rides her pony, Macaroni.

Life in the White House

The White House has 132 rooms, including a bowling alley and a movie theater. Its huge staff includes chefs, housekeepers, and even a full-time doctor.

First families find ways to make the White House feel like home. Jimmy Carter (1977–1981) had a treehouse built for his daughter, Amy. Bill Clinton (1993–2001) created a music room where he could practice the saxophone. And many presidents keep pets. Calvin Coolidge (1923–1929) had a raccoon named Rebecca.

The White House has 147 windows. Imagine keeping them all clean!

Getting Around

A president travels in style and safety. On the ground, the president rides in a limousine that's as strong as a tank. For longer trips, the president flies in the Air Force One jet. It has high-tech equipment and 85 phones!

Even presidents need a break. They can visit Camp David, a cabin in Maryland. And many presidents go on vacations. Wherever the president and first family go, Secret Service agents protect them.

Some people thought President Theodore Roosevelt (1901–1909) took too much time off. This cartoon shows him running off to his vacation cabin. How much time off do you think presidents should be able to take?

A Role That Matters

Since the U.S. government was established some 230 years ago, thousands of Americans have run for president.

Though many drop out of the race along the way, dozens have been elected to the office and served. Some even served more than one term. Each of these presidents brought a unique perspective to the highest office in the land. Each made decisions that have shaped our country in every possible aspect and, in turn, our everyday lives. This is why the presidency matters.

Thank You, Presidents

This chart shows some of the ways that presidents' decisions have affected your everyday life.

Every time you . . .	You should think of . . .	Why?
Play or go to school instead of working in a factory	Franklin D. Roosevelt (1933–1945)	He signed the Fair Labor Standards Act, which put strict rules on how and when children could work.
Use a toy or other product without being hurt	Richard M. Nixon (1969–1974)	He signed a law setting up the Consumer Product Safety Commission. It makes sure products sold in the United States are safe.
Visit a national park	Ulysses S. Grant (1869–1877)	He created the country's first national park, Yellowstone National Park. Many other parks would follow.
Go on a long road trip with your family	Dwight D. Eisenhower (1953–1961)	He established the interstate highway system.
Cuddle a teddy bear	Theodore "Teddy" Roosevelt (1901–1909)	He got national attention when he decided not to shoot at a bear while on a hunting trip. Afterward, a toy maker made a stuffed bear and named it for the president. It was the first teddy bear!

Mount Rushmore in South Dakota honors presidents George Washington, Thomas Jefferson, Theodore Roosevelt, and Abraham Lincoln.

George Washington
1789–1797

John Adams
1797–1801

Thomas Jefferson
1801–1809

James Madison
1809–1817

John Tyler
1841–1845

James K. Polk
1845–1849

Zachary Taylor
1849–1850

Millard Fillmore
1850–1853

Rutherford B. Hayes
1877–1881

James Garfield
1881

Chester A. Arthur
1881–1885

Grover Cleveland
1885–1889

Woodrow Wilson
1913–1921

Warren G. Harding
1921–1923

Calvin Coolidge
1923–1929

Herbert Hoover
1929–1933

Richard M. Nixon
1969–1974

Gerald R. Ford
1974–1977

James Carter
1977–1981

Ronald Reagan
1981–1989

Presidents

Take a look at each of the leaders who has served as President of the United States.

James Monroe
1817–1825

John Quincy Adams
1825–1829

Andrew Jackson
1829–1837

Martin Van Buren
1837–1841

William Henry Harrison
1841

Franklin Pierce
1853–1857

James Buchanan
1857–1861

Abraham Lincoln
1861–1865

Andrew Johnson
1865–1869

Ulysses S. Grant
1869–1877

Benjamin Harrison
1889–1893

Grover Cleveland
1893–1897

William McKinley
1897–1901

Theodore Roosevelt
1901–1909

William H. Taft
1909–1913

Franklin D. Roosevelt
1933–1945

Harry S. Truman
1945–1953

Dwight D. Eisenhower
1953–1961

John F. Kennedy
1961–1963

Lyndon B. Johnson
1963–1969

George H. W. Bush
1989–1993

William J. Clinton
1993–2001

George W. Bush
2001–2009

Barack Obama
2009–2017

Donald J. Trump
2017–

Getting the President's Attention

Through history, kids like you have shared their views with the president.

One example is the March of the Mill Children. In 1903, one in six kids worked in factories, mines, and farms. They faced many dangers. A group of child factory workers decided to march from Pennsylvania to New York, where President Teddy Roosevelt was staying. Their march drew attention to the issue of child labor. Years later, under President Franklin Roosevelt, laws were passed to stop it.

The young marchers thought kids belonged in school, not factories.

In the 1950s and 1960s, kids took action on another issue. Some states did not allow black people and white people to go to the same restaurants or other places. This was called segregation. To fight it, some African American kids participated in sit-ins. They went to restaurants open only to white customers. They sat and asked to be served. Over time, such actions brought change. In 1964, President Lyndon B. Johnson (1963–1969) signed a law ending segregation.

Get Involved!

You may be too young to vote for president, but there is still plenty you can do to be an active citizen. Try taking these steps:

Learn about important issues in the nation by reading the news.

Talk to others about the issues. Ask questions to understand their point of view.

Help your community. Try to make changes that will make it a better place.

Make your voice heard by writing to local, state, and national leaders. You can write to the president at the address below. Be sure to include your address. You might get a letter back!

The White House
1600 Pennsylvania Avenue NW
Washington, DC 20500

Did you find the truth?

T One president kept a pet raccoon at the White House.

F You can run for president once you turn 21 years old.

Resources

The book you just read is a first introduction to the presidency, and to the history and government of our country. There is always more to learn and discover. In addition to this title, we encourage you to seek out complementary resources.

Other books in this series:

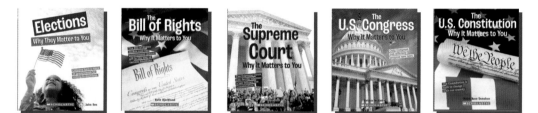

You can also look at:

Bausum, Ann. *Our Country's Presidents: A Complete Encyclopedia of the U.S. Presidency*. Washington, DC: National Geographic, 2017.

Jackson, Carolyn. *The Election Book: The People Pick a President*. New York: Scholastic, 2012.

Roosevelt, Eleanor, with Michelle Markel. *When You Grow Up to Vote*. New York: Roaring Brook Press, 2018.

Sullivan, George. *Scholastic Book of Presidents*. New York: Scholastic, 2016.

Glossary

address (uh-DRESS) a prepared speech

ambassadors (am-BASS-uh-durz) people sent by a country's government to represent it in another country

bills (BILZ) written plans for a new law, to be debated and passed by a body of legislators

campaign (kam-PAYN) to organize activities in an effort to achieve a goal, such as getting elected to office

diplomat (DIP-luh-mat) someone who officially represents their country's government in a foreign country as a job

electoral votes (uh-LEK-tor-uhl VOHTS) votes that a group of people cast based on who the majority of citizens voted for in their state

federal (FED-ur-uhl) national; describing a system of government in which states are united under a central authority

inauguration (in-aw-gyuh-RAY-shuhn) the ceremony of swearing in a public official

pardon (PARD-uhn) to forgive or excuse someone

term (TURM) a definite or limited period of time

treaties (TREE-teez) formal agreements between two or more countries

veto (VEE-toh) to stop a bill from becoming a law

Index

Page numbers in **bold** indicate illustrations.

About the Author

Karen Kellaher is an editor in Scholastic's classroom magazine division and has written more than 20 books for kids and teachers. She holds a bachelor's degree in communications from the University of Scranton (Pennsylvania) and a master's degree combining elementary education and publishing from New York University's Gallatin School of Individualized Study.